# AN UNDERTOW OF SHARKS
## AND OTHER NEW GROUPS!

**W. W. ROWE**

Illustrated by Charles A. Filius

CHARWOOD
PUBLICATIONS

## An Undertow of Sharks
## and Other New Groups
Copyright © 2013 by W. W. Rowe & Charles A. Filius

Published by
**Charwood Publications**
P. O. Box 14881
Long Beach, CA 90853

Book design & production by C. A. Filius

All Rights Reserved.
Printed in the United States of America.
No part of this book may be used or reproduced
in any manner whatsoever without written permission.

ISBN-13: 978-0-9910347-0-3
ISBN-10: 0991034708
LCCN: 2013953766

For Eleanor
W. W. R.


In Loving Memory of
**Denise Perrella**
An Angel Here, An Angel There
C. A. F.

Who doesn't know a herd of donkeys? A school of fish? A colony of ants?

You may also be familiar with a plague of locusts. A pride of lions. Or even an exaltation of larks.

We need some new and improved groups. Far-out groups! Astonishing, humorous groups!

# AN UNDERTOW OF SHARKS

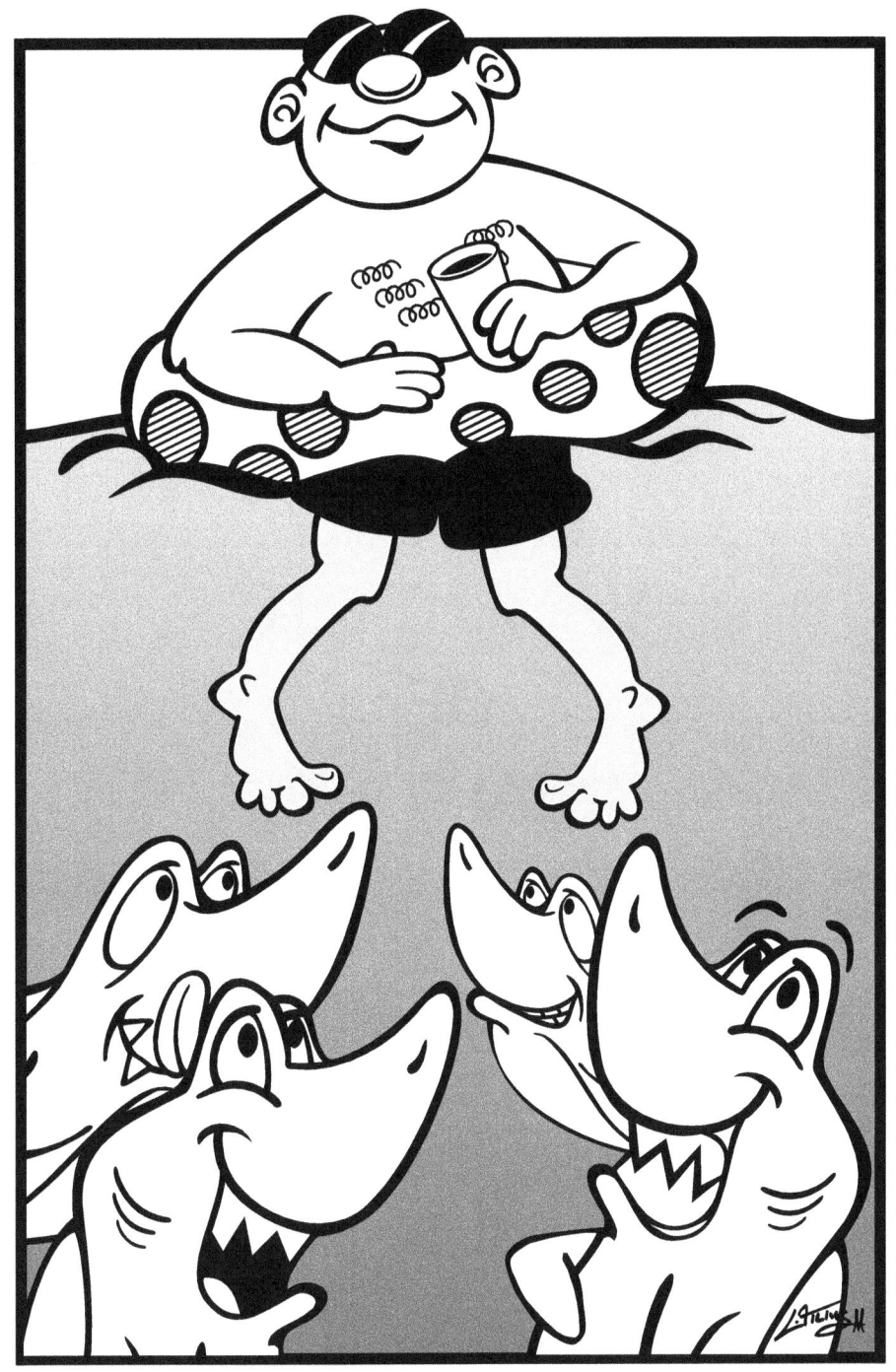

# A VACANT LOT OF REALTORS

# A WILD BUNCH OF FLORISTS

# A CONGREGATION OF SINNERS

# A PEW OF STRUGGLING DEODORANTS

# A HORDE OF MISERS

# A DROVE OF USED CARS

# AN EMBARRASSMENT OF BRITCHES

# A PANTING OF WATCHDOGS

# A STACK OF BRASSIERES

# A RUN OF JAILBREAKS

# A SLEW OF AXE-MURDERS

# A SILLINESS OF SUPERSTITIONS

# A RAFT OF CANOES

# A HANDFUL OF GROPERS

# A HERD OF EAVESDROPPERS

# A POOL OF PLUMBERS

# A SCRAMBLE OF EASTER-EGG HUNTERS

# A BUFFET LINE OF BEDBUGS

# A HOT BATCH OF BAKERS

# A HOBBLE OF LAME EXCUSES

A
BOREDOM
OF
NEWS
ALERTS

# A PACK OF CARDSHARPS

# A SERENDIPITY OF APPETIZERS

# A CLIQUE OF COMPUTER HACKERS

# A CACHE OF COUNTERFEITERS

# A STAGGERING OF ZOMBIES

# A SLEEPINESS OF YAWNS

# A
# HEAP
# OF
# WRESTLERS

# AN EMERGENCY ROOM OF MUMMIES

# A LURKING OF SPIES

# A FLOCK OF SUCKERS

# AN EXPLOSION OF ARMS RACES

# A HOST OF GUESTS

# A FULLNESS OF MOTELS

# A TIGHTWAD OF BANKERS

# A FEAST OF WEIGHT-LOSS PROGRAMS

# A STRING OF GUITARISTS

# A CHORUS OF STOOL PIDGEONS

# AN ARMY OF PACIFISTS

# A TANGLE OF HAIRDRESSERS

# A CLUB OF CAVEMEN

# A CONFUSION OF RESTROOMS

# A GLOOMINESS OF DOOMSAYERS

# A PLAGUE OF DOCTORS

# A FLEET OF TURTLES

# A HORROR OF KETCHUP STAINS

# A MURKINESS OF MARTINIS

# A MORASS OF NUDISTS

# A TITILLATION OF GIRLY MAGAZINES

# A FIRING LINE OF ACCUSATORY FINGERS

# A MIXTURE OF BARTENDERS

# A FURTIVENESS OF FARTS

# A RING OF JEWELERS

# A JUMBLE OF ORGANIZERS

# A SYMMETRY OF TWINS

# A PRETZEL OF YOGA POSTURES

# A ZOMBIENESS OF SLEEPWALKERS

# AN UPRISING OF BALLOONS

# A CAULDRON OF GRUDGES

# A GATHERING OF STAMP COLLECTORS

# AN ALLIANCE OF TRAITORS

# A CLUSTER OF VINEYARDS

# A SOCIETY OF HERMITS

# A KINDERGARTEN OF CONGRESSMEN

# A PATCH OF PIRATES

# AN ARRAY OF SUNBATHERS

# A ZOO OF PROTESTERS

# A HELPFUL LIST OF SIDE EFFECTS

# A SWARM OF AUNTS

# A POTLUCK OF CANNIBALS

# A SECRECY OF UNDERCOVER AGENTS

# A SPIRITING OF GHOSTS

# A COMBINATION OF PADLOCKS

# A CONCENTRATION OF HYPNOTISTS

# A GAUNTLET OF PICKPOCKETS

# A MENAGERIE OF FOOTBALL FANS

# A PARADISE OF GAMBLERS

# A MINEFIELD OF MICROPHONES

# AN EARRING OF GOSSIPS

# A NONEXISTENCE OF UNICORNS

## ABOUT THE AUTHOR

W.W. Rowe is the author of seven books about Russian literature. His numerous children's books include **Amy and Gully in Rainbowland** and **Amy and Gully with Aliens** (Snow Lion Publications) and **Clever Billy** (Sanctuary Publications). He lives in Sedona, Arizona with his writer-artist wife, Eleanor, and their imperious dachshund, Princess Ozma.

## ABOUT THE ARTIST

Charles A. Filius is a highly acclaimed medium, cartoonist and author. He has written two books on his spiritual experiences. His first book, **Selections from On A Wing & A Prayer,** was published in 2007. His second, **Dailies**, was published in 2011. **An Undertow of Sharks** is his eighth collaboration with author W. W. Rowe.

His cartooning work has been widely published throughout his 25 year career. In addition to self-syndicating a single panel comic, **Paradox Found**, in the late 90's, he also created the acclaimed adoption-themed strip, **Is It Mine?** which touted the perspective of closed adoption records through the eyes of the adult adoptee. Charles continually tours the country sharing his own spiritual experiences with others through his humorous and inspirational writings, drawings and seminars, which are often standing room only. He has been a proud member of the National Cartoonists' Society since 1995.

## ALSO BY FILIUS & ROWE
### Available through Charwood Publications

## CLEVER BILLY
### AND OTHER
### FREAKY, FUNNY LIMERICKS
### $12.95

ISBN: 978-0-9785334-1-0

## THE FLAW
## OF KARMA
### $12.95

ISBN: 978-0-9785334-2-7

### CHARWOOD
### PUBLICATIONS
www.CharwoodPublications.com

## ALSO BY FILIUS & ROWE
Available through Charwood Publications

# THE SECRET LIFE OF THINGS

$12.95

ISBN: 978-0-9830018-1-2

# THINGS ALIVE!
AND OTHER
FREAKY SECRETS
$12.95

ISBN: 978-0-615-66672-3

**PUBLICATIONS**
www.CharwoodPublications.com

## ALSO BY FILIUS & ROWE
### Available through Charwood Publications

### THE WIZARD'S WAYWARD WAND

$12.95

ISBN: 978-0-9843754-0-0

### THE WAND GOES WILD

$12.95

ISBN: 978-0-9843754-4-8

### CHARWOOD PUBLICATIONS
www.CharwoodPublications.com

## ALSO BY FILIUS & ROWE
Available through Charwood Publications

## THE WAND IS WENDY!

$12.95

ISBN: 978-0-9830018-8-1

## CHARWOOD PUBLICATIONS
www.CharwoodPublications.com

www.ingramcontent.com/pod-product-compliance
Lightning Source LLC
Chambersburg PA
CBHW061650040426
42446CB00010B/1664